Three Lectures on the Rate of Wages: With a Preface on the Causes and Remedies of the Present Disturbances
Nassau Senior

Prism Key Press, 2013.
New York, NY.

www.PrismKeyPress.com

ISBN-13: 978-1490937397
ISBN-10: 1490937390

Three Lectures on the Rate of Wages:
With a Preface on the Causes and Remedies of the Present Disturbances

Nassau Senior

TABLE OF CONTENTS

Preface 7
LECTURE I: Definition of High and Low Wages 20
LECTURE II: Popular Errors on the Causes Affecting Wages 29
LECTURE III: Popular Errors On the Causes Affecting Wages, (cncld.) 41

Preface

The following Lectures contain little that is not well known to many of my readers, and still less that is peculiarly and exclusively appropriate to the present emergency. They were written and delivered in a period of profound tranquillity; but we are now in a state which may require the exertions of every individual among the educated classes, and many may have to assist in executing, or even in originating measures for the relief of the labouring population, who are not yet sufficiently familiar with the principles according to which that relief is to be afforded.

Under such circumstances, it has appeared to me that advantage might be derived from a short explanation of the ambiguities and fallacies which most obscure the subject of wages — the most difficult and the most important of all the branches of political economy.

My principal object, however, has been to draw attention to the elementary proposition, that *the rate of wages depends on the extent of the fund for the maintenance of labourers, compared with the number of labourers to be maintained.* This proposition is so nearly self-evident, that it may appear scarcely to deserve a formal statement; still less to be dwelt on as if it were a discovery. It is true that it is obvious and trite; but, perhaps, on that very account, its practical consequences have been neglected. In the first place, if this proposition be admitted, many prevalent opinions respecting the effects of unproductive consumption, of machinery, and of free-trade, must be abandoned; and to show this, is the object of the second and third of the following Lectures. And in the second place, it must also follow that the rate of wages can be raised, or, what is nearly the same, the condition of the labouring classes improved, only by either increasing the fund for their maintenance, or diminishing the number to be maintained.

The principal means by which-the fund for the maintenance of labourers can be increased, is by increasing the productiveness of labour. And this may be done, —

First, By allowing every man to exert himself in the way which, from experience, he finds most beneficial; by freeing industry from the mass of restrictions, prohibitions, and protecting duties, with which the Legislature, sometimes in well-meaning. ignorance, sometimes in pity, and sometimes in national jealousy, has laboured to crush or misdirect her efforts; and,

Secondly, By putting an end to that unhappy system which, in the southern counties, has dissociated labour from subsistence—has madd wades not a matter of contract between the master and the workman, but a right in the one, and a tax on the other; and, by removing the motives for exertion, has rendered, as far as it has been possible, the labourer unworthy of his hire.

The only effectual and permanent means of preventing the undue increase of the number to be maintained, is to raise the moral and intellectual character of the labouring population; to improve, or, I fear we must say, to create habits of prudence, of self-respect, and of self-restraint; to equalize, as by nature they are equal, the wages of the single and the married, and no longer to make a family the passport to allowance. But these are necessarily gradual measures — they are preventive, not remedial. The only immediate remedy for an actual excess in one class of the population, is the ancient and approved one, *coloniam deducere*.

It is of great importance to keep in mind, that not only is emigration the sole immediate remedy, but that it is a remedy preparatory to the adoption and necessary to the safety of every other.

The principal cause the calamities that we are witnessing, has been the disturbance which the poor-laws, as at present administered in the south of England, have created in the most extensive and the most important of all political relations, the relation between the employer and the labourer.

The slave (using that word in its strict sense) cannot choose his owner, his employment, or his residence; his whole services are the property of another, and their value, however high, gives him no additional claim. On the other hand, he is entitled to subsistence for himself and his family: clothing, lodging, food, medical attendance — everything, in short, which is necessary to keep him in health and strength is provided for him, from the same motives, and with the same liberality, that they are provided for the other domestic animals of his master. He is *bound* to labour, and has a *right* to be maintained. Extreme idleness may subject him to the lash, but extraordinary diligence cannot better his condition. He is equally incapable of being benefited by self-restraint, or injured by improvidence. While single, he receives a bare subsistence; if he have a family, his maintenance rises in precise proportion to his wants: the prudential check to population does not exist — it is kept down, if at all, by oppression on the part of the master, or vice on that of the slave. This, notwithstanding the various degrees of mitigation which have been introduced by custom or by law, is in substance the condition of slaves, wherever slavery exists.

In such a country distress begins, not, as in the case of a free country, with the lower orders, but with the higher. A bad system, therefore, can continue there much longer, because the class affected have farther to fall; and, for the same reason, the ruin, when it does come, is sudden and irretrievable. While misgovernment, by excessive or ill-placed taxation, by commercial restrictions, by allowing insecurity of person or property, by applying any artificial stimulus to population, or under any other of its. numerous forms, is gradually wasting the surplus that belongs to landlords and capitalists, the slave population may scarcely feel its effects. Subsistence is all they are entitled to, and that they must receive as long as their labour produces it. But the instant that surplus is gone, and distress reaches those whose previous maintenance was only equal to their necessities, what is there between them and absolute destruction? If the evils which have been so long accumulating in some of our West Indian islands had affected a free country, the whole population would, long ago, have risen to redress them. But as yet, they have reached only the slave-owner. He has found his property gradually wasting away; he has found that his slaves every year consume a larger and a larger proportion of what they produce; but even still he has something to lose: and while that is the case, *their* situation is unaffected. When the whole produce has become only sufficient to feed the negroes, — a time which, under the present system, is rapidly advancing in some of the older islands, — the whites must abandon them as a field for all the moral and physical evil that slaves, helpless by education and desperate from want, will mutually suffer and inflict[1]

    The freeman (using that term in its full meaning,) is the master of his exertions, and of his residence. He may refuse to quit the spot, or to change the employment, in which his labour has become unprofitable. As he may refuse to labour at all, be may ask for his services Whatever remuneration he thinks fit; but as no one is bound to purchase those services, and as no one is obliged to afford him food, clothing, or any of the necessaries of life, he is forced, if he would subsist, to follow the trade, and dwell in the place, and exert the diligence which will make his services worth purchasing; and he is forced to offer them for sale, by the same necessity which forces the capitalist to offer him wages in exchange for them. And the bargain is settled, like all other free bargains, by the respective market values of the things exchanged. As marriage has no tendency .to increase the value of his labour, it has no tendency to increase his remuneration. He defers it, therefore, till the savings made while he was single afford a fund to meet the expenses of a family; and population is kept down by the only check that is consistent with moral or physical welfare — the prudential check:

To this state of things there is a near approach among the labouring classes in the most advanced districts of the continent of Europe, in the lowlands of Scotland, and even throughout the British empire, among the best educated of those classes who derive their chief subsistence from their exertions, including professional persons, domestic servants, skilled artisans, and that portion of the shopkeepers whose profits are, in fact, principally the wages of their labour.

The poor-laws, as administered in the southern districts of England, are an attempt to unite the irreconcilable advantages of freedom and servitude. The labourer is to be a free agent, but without the hazards of free agency; to be free from the coercion, but to enjoy the assured subsistence of the slave. He is expected to be diligent, though he has no fear of want; provident, though his pay rises as his family increases; attached to a master who employs him in pursuance of a vestry resolution; and grateful for the allowance which the magistrates order him as a right.

In the natural state of the relation between the capitalist and the labourer, when the amount of wages to be paid, and of work to be done, are the subjects of a free and open bargain; when the labourer obtains, and knows that he is to obtain just what his services are worth to his employer, he must feel any fall in the price of his labour to be an evil, but is not likely to complain of it as an injustice. Greater exertion and severer economy are his first resources in distress; and what they cannot supply, he receives with gratitude from the benevolent. The connexion between him and his master has the kindliness of a voluntary association, in which each party is conscious of benefit, and each feels that his own welfare depends, to a certain extent, on the welfare of the other. But the instant wages cease to be a bargain — the instant the labourer is paid, not according to his value, but his wants, he ceases to be a freeman. He acquires the indolence, the improvidence, the rapacity, and the malignity, but not the subordination of a slave. He is told that he has a *right* to wages, but that he is *bound* to work? Who is to decide how hard he ought to work, or how hard he does work? Who is to decide what amount of wages he has a *right* to? As yet, the decision has been made by the overseers and the magistrates. But they were interested parties. The labourer has thought fit to correct that decision. For the present he thinks that he has a *right* to 2s. 3d. a day in winter, and 2s. 6d. in summer. And our only hope seems to be, that the promise of such wages will bribe him into quiet. But who can doubt that he will measure his rights by his wishes, or that his wishes will extend with the prospect of their gratification? The present tide may not complete the inundation, but it will be a dreadful error if we mistake the ebb for a permanent receding of the waters. A breach has been made in the seawall, and with every succeeding irruption they will swell higher and spread more widely. What we are suffering is nothing to what we have to expect. Next year, perhaps, the labourer will think it unjust that he should have less than 4s. a day in winter, and 5s. in summer; — and woe to the tyrants who deny him his right!

It is true, that such a right could not be permanently enforced; — it is true, that if the labourer burns the corn-ricks in which his subsistence for the current year is stored — if he consumes in idleness or in riot the time and the exertions on which next year's harvest depends — if he wastes in extravagant wages, or drives to foreign countries, the capital that is to assist and render productive his labour, he will be the greatest sufferer in the common ruin. Those who have property may escape with a portion of it to some country in which their rights will be protected; but the labourer must remain to enjoy his own works—to feel that the real rewards for plunder and devastation are want and disease.

But have the consequences of the present. system ever been explained to the labourer? Is not his right to good wages. re-echoed from all parts of the country Is he not told — 'Dwell in the land, and verily thou shall be fed?' Does not the Honourable Member who has affixed this motto to his work, assume, that the fund out of which the labourer is to be fed is practically inexhaustible? And can words more strongly imply that his sufferings arise from the *injustice* of his superiors? Have not even magistrates and landlords recommended the destruction, or, what is the same, both in principle aud effect, the disuse of the very machines of which the object is to render labour more efficient in the production of the articles consumed by the labourer — in the production of that very fund on the extent of which, compared with the number to. be maintained, the amount of wages depends? And is there any real difference between this conduct and the burning of a rick-yard? Threshing-machines are the present objects of hostility, ploughs will be the next; spades will then be found to diminish employment; and when it has been made penal to give advantage to labour by any tool or instrument Whatever, the last step must be to prohibit the use of the right-hand.

Have sufficient pains been taken even to expose the absurdity of what appears so obvious to the populace — that the landlords ought to reduce their rents and the clergy their tithe, and then the farmer would give better wages? If the farmer had his land for nothing, still it would not be his interest to give any man more wages for a day's work than his day's work was worth. He could .better afford it, no doubt, to be paid as a tax; but why should the farmer pay that tax more than the physician or the shopkeeper? If the farmer is to employ, at this advanced rate of wages, only whom he chooses, the distress will be increased, since he wil! employ only that smaller number whose labour is worth their increased pay. If he is to employ a certain proportion of the labourers, however numerous, in his parish, he is, in fact, to pay rent and tithes as before, with this difference only, that they are to be paid to paupers, instead of to the landlord and the parson; and that the payment is not a fixed but an indefinite sum, and a sum which must every year increase. in an accelerated ratio, as the increase of population rushes to fill up this new vacuum, till rent, tithes, profit, and capital, are all eaten up, and pauperism produces what may be called its natural effects — for they are the effects which, if unchecked, it must ultimately produce—famine, pestilence, and civil war.

That this country can preserve its prosperity, or even its social existence, if the state of feeling which I have described becomes universal among the. lower classes,. I think no one will be bold enough to maintain. That it is extensively prevalent, and that, under the present administration of the poor-laws, it *will*, at no remote period, become universal in the southern districts, appears to me to be equally clear. But who, in the present state of those districts, will venture to carry into execution a real and effectual alteration of the poor-laws? Remove, by emigration, the pauperism that now oppresses those districts, and such an alteration, though it may remain difficult, will cease to be impracticable.

Again, the corn-laws, by their tendency to raise the price of subsistence, by the ruin which they have inflicted on the internal corn-trade, and the stimulus which they have given to the increase of the agricultural population, have without doubt been amongst the causes of the present distress; and if, while the population of England and Wales continues to increase *at the rate of 500 persons a day*, the introduction of foreign corn is subject, under ordinary prices, to a prohibitive duty, those laws will become every day more mischievous, and less remediable. But the repeal of those laws, however gradual (and only a gradual repeal can be thought of), would, under the present pressure of pauperism, tend to aggravate the agricultural distress. Lighten that pressure, and we may gradually revert to the only safe system—the system of freedom.

This observation, indeed, is only one example of a general rule. Nature has decreed that the road to good shall be through evil — that no improvement shall take place in which the general advantage shall not be accompanied by partial suffering. The obvious remedy is to remove those whose labour has ceased to be profitable, to a country that will afford room for their exertions. Few inventions, during the present century, have conferred greater benefits on the labouring classes than that of the power-loom. By diminishing the expense of clothing, it has been a source, not merely of comfort, but of health and longevity. But its proximate effect was to spread ruin among the hand-weavers; to reduce almost all of them to a mere subsistence, and many to the most abject want. Ever since its introduction, thousands have been pining away under misery, not alleviated even by hope; with no rational expectation, but that the ensuing year would be more calamitous than the passing one: and this without fault, without even improvidence.' If it had been thought that the removal of a fellow-creature from misery to happiness is worth £12, they might now have formed a flourishing settlement in British America.

The hostility of many, coupled with the indifference of almost all others, to any systematic plan of emigration, is a ground for regret and alarm, considered not only as a cause, but as a symptom. It is a lamentable proof of ignorance as to the real state of .the country, or of carelessness as to its welfare, or of a determination to make no sacrifice for its relief.

We are told that emigration would be expensive, and again we are told that the vacuum would be filled up.

It is true, that to remove a million of persons might, perhaps, cost £12,000,000 sterling; that is to say, might cost as much as the direct expenditure of **three months war**; and that an expenditure of £12,000,000 sterling is an evil. But in the first place, it has been demonstrated[2] that the expense of keeping paupers at home is far greater than that of their removal. It may be necessary to repeat, though it has often been remarked before, that the relief is afforded not only to those individuals who emigrate, but to the much greater number who remain. If there are 450 labourers in a district which requires the full employment, and affords the full subsistence of only 400, all, or nearly all, will be in distress, and by the emigration of fifty all will be relieved. And, in the second place, even if the balance of expense were on the side of removing a portion of our surplus population, is no expense beyond that of their mere keep to be feared from their presence? If the present insurrection spread (and it will spread if the peasantry are told, as. practically they have been told, that for riot and rebellion three days' imprisonment is the punishment, and a rise of wages the **reward**); if the ravage of the country reacts, as it will react, on the towns; if, when trade begins to languish, the master manufacturers, according to their late practice, dismiss their workmen, and the manufacturing workmen, in their turn, destroy machinery; if the foundations, not merely of our wealth, but of our existence, are thus impaired, will twelve millions, or twenty millions, or even a hundred millions sterling represent the loss?

It is true, that if we adopt to preventive measures, if we persist blindly in our course of error, the temporary relief afforded by emigration will come to an end, and the vacuum will, in sixteen or seventeen years, be filled up. But is it certain that we shall not profit by experience? Have we a right, or, rather, are we compelled, to assume, as a link in the argument, that we and our successors must be madmen ? If a man has been outrunning his income, is it quite certain that we can do him no good by paying his debts, on the ground that if he goes on in the same thoughtless expenditure, he will again be involved as deeply as ever? And even granting that the vacuum will be filled up, will it be nothing to have obtained sixteen years' respite? — to have weathered the existing storm? — to have adjourned the crisis to a period which may be more favourable, and cannot possibly be less so?

We are told that the labourers form the strength of the country, and that to diminish their number is to incur voluntary feebleness. But does the pauper, — the man whose labour is not worth his subsistence, who consumes more than he produces,— does he add to the strength of the country? When I hear such remarks, I fancy myself standing by the bedside of au apoplectic patient, and hearing the nurse and the friends prohibit the lancet. 'The blood,' says one, 'is the support of life: how can you think of diminishing it in his present state of weakness?' 'If you do diminish it,' cries out another, ' with his habits of free living, it will be renewed; in a year the vacuum will be filled up.' But is it impossible that the blood can be in excess? Is it certain that his habits are unchangeable? Shall we let him die low, lest we should have to bleed him again a year hence?

It will be observed, that I have assumed that the paupers are willing to emigrate. That they have been so as yet, is unquestionable: I hope, I had almost said I trust, that they still continue to be so. But if they are allowed. to fix the labour they are to give, and the wages they are to receive; if they are to help themselves, while it lasts, from the whole property of the country, it is too much to expect that they will not prefer idleness, riot, and plunder at home, to subsistence, however ample, to be earned by toil and hardship abroad. But this only shows the danger, the madness of delay. While we are deliberating, or even before we have begun to deliberate, 'the moment for applying the remedy is passing away.

Hitherto, it has been common to defend every existing practice as agreeable to common sense, in opposition to the visionary schemes of political theorists; to. plead experience in behalf of everything that has long prevailed, and to deprecate new experiments. It is high time that those who profess to venerate experience should now, at length, show that they can learn from it. To what has common prejudice, reigning under the title of common sense, brought us? Have the *practical* men who have hitherto administered our system of poor-laws saved us from being brought to the very brink of ruin? Or have they suggested any effectual means for stopping our downward career? Surely common sense, if there be any such thing in the country, will now, at last, bear witness to the truth of Bacon's maxim, that he who dreads new remedies, must expect new evils!'

Lincoln's Inn, December 3, 1830.

Notes

1. This is one of the modes in which slavery may be extinguished, but it is a dreadful abuse of language to call it euthanasia.
2. See Mr. Wilmot Horton's 'Causes and Remedies of Pauperism,' fourth series.

Hie etiam fatis aperit Cassandra futuris
Ora Dei jussu non unquam credita Teucris.

LECTURE I: Definition of High and Low Wages

The labourers form the mass of every community. The inquiry into the causes affecting wages is, therefore, the most important branch of political economy. In the following Lectures I propose, first, to explain some ambiguities in the terms high and low wages; secondly, to state the proximate cause which regulates the amount of wages; and lastly, to expose some prevalent errors respecting that cause; leaving the remoter causes, the cause of the proximate cause, for discussion in a subsequent course.

Wages are the remuneration received by the labourer in recompense for having exerted his faculties of mind and body; and they are termed high or low, in proportion to the extent of that remuneration. That extent has been estimated by three different measures; and the words high and low wages have, consequently, been used in three different senses.

First. Wages have been termed high or low, according to the amount of *money* earned by the labourer within a given period, without any reference to the commodities which that money would purchase; as when we say that wages have risen since the reign of Henry VII, because the labourer now receives 1 s. 6d. or 2.s. a day, and then received only 4½d.

Secondly. They have been termed high or low, according to the quantity and quality of the commodities obtained by the labourer, without any reference to his receipts in money; as when we say that wages have fallen since the reign of Henry VII, because the labourer then earned two pecks of wheat a day, and now earns only one.

Thirdly. They have been termed high or low, according to the share or proportion which the labourer receives of the produce of his own labour, without any reference to the total amount of that produce.

The first nomenclature, that which measures wages simply by their amount in money, is the popular one. The second, that which considers wages simply with reference to the quantity and quality of the commodities received by the labourer, or to speak more correctly, purchaseable with his money wages, was that generally adopted by Adam Smith. The third, that which considers wages as high or low, simply with reference to the labourer's share or proportion of what he produces, was introduced by Mr. Ricardo, and has been continued by many of his followers.

This last use of the words high and low wages has always appeared to me one of the most unfortunate of Mr. Ricardo's many innovations in the language of political economy. In the first place, it has a tendency to withdraw our attention, even when we arc considering the subject of wages, from the facts which most influence the labourer's condition. To ascertain whether his wages are high or low, we are desired to inquire, not whether he is ill or well paid, — not whether he is well or ill fed, or clothed, or lodged, or warmed, but simply what proportion of what he produces comes to his share. During the last four or five years, many a hand-weaver has received only 8s. 3d. for producing, by a fortnight's exertion, a web that the capitalist has sold for 8s. 4d. A coal-merchant often pays his men two guineas a week, and charges his employers for their services two guineas and a half. But, according to Mr. Ricardo's nomenclature, the wages of the weaver, at 4s. 1½d. a week, are much higher than those of the coal-heaver at two guineas, since the weaver receives 99 per cent of the value of his labour, while the coal heaver had only 80 per cent.

And, even if the nomenclature in question were free from this objection — even if the point on which it endeavours to fix the attention were the most important, instead of being the least important. incident to wages, it still would be inconvenient from its obscurity. No writer can hope to be consistent in the use of familiar words in a sense always different from their established meaning, and often directly opposed to it; still less can he hope to be always understood. Even Mr. Ricardo, though he professes to mean by high wages a great proportion, has in several places considered them as productive of consequences which would follow only if they signified a great amount. And his followers and opponents have, almost uniformly, supposed those words to mean a great amount. Since the publication of Mr. Ricardo's work, it has been received as an axiom, among the dabblers in political economy, that, according to the established doctrines of the science, high wages and high profits are incompatible; and, therefore, that either the leading doctrines of political economy are false, or the interests. of the labourer and the capitalist are always directly opposed to one another. The former opinion has been adopted by the large class who do not attend to what they read; the latter, by the still larger class who do not attend to what they see.

The two other meanings of the words high and low wages, that which refers to the money, and that which refers to the commodities, received by the labourer, are both equally convenient, if we consider the rate of wages *at the same time and place*; for then they both mean the same thing. At the same time and place, the labourer who receives the highest wages necessarily receives the most commodities. But when we refer to different places, or different times, the words high or low wages direct the attention to very different subjects, as we understand them to mean more or less in money, or more or less in commodities. The differences which have taken place in the amount of money wages at different times, inform us of scarcely any thing but the abundance or scarcity of the precious metals at those times: facts which are seldom of much importance. The differences in the amount of money wages in different places at the same time, are of much more importance, since they indicate the different values of the labour of different countries in the general market of the world. But even these differences afford no premises, from which the positive condition of the labouring classes, in any country, can be inferred, and but imperfect grounds for estimating their relative condition. The only data which enable us to ascertain the actual situation of the labourers at any given time and place, or their comparative situation of different times and places, are the quantity and quality of the commodities which form their wages, if paid in kind, or are purchaseable with their wages, if paid in money. And as the actual or comparative situation of the labourer is the principal object of the following inquiry, I shall use the word wages, to express, not the money, but the commodities, which the labourer receives; and I shall consider wages to rise as the quantity or quality of those commodities is increased or improved, and to fall as that quantity or quality is diminished or deteriorated.

It is obvious, too, that the labourer's situation does not depend on the amount which he receives at any one time, but on his average receipts during a given period — during a week, a month, or a year; and that the longer the period taken, the more accurate will be the estimate. Weekly wages have, of course, more tendency to equality than daily ones, and annual than monthly; and, if we could ascertain the amount earned by a man during five, or ten, or twenty years, we should know his situation better than if we confined our attention to a single year. There is, however, so much difficulty in ascertaining the amount of wages during very long periods, that, I think, a single year will be the best that we can take. It comprehends what, in most climates, are very different, summer and winter wages; it comprehends also the period during which the most important vegetable productions come to maturity in temperate climates, and on that account has generally been adopted by political economists as the average period for which capital is supposed to be advanced.

I should observe, that I include, as part of the wages of the married labourer, those of his wife and unemancipated children. To omit them would lead to inaccurate estimates of the comparative situation of the labourers in different countries, or in different occupations. In those employments which are carried on under shelter, and with the assistance of that machinery which affords power, and requires human aid only for its direction, the industry of a woman, or a child, approaches in efficiency to that of a full-grown man. A girl of fourteen can manage a power-loom nearly as well as her father; but where strength, or exposure to the seasons, are required, little can be done by the wife, or the girls, or even by the boys, until they approach the age at which they usually quit their father's house. The earnings of the wife and children of many a Manchester weaver or spinner exceed, or equal, those of himself. Those of the wife and children of an agricultural labourer, or of a carpenter, or coal-heaver, are generally unimportant — while the husband, in each case, receive 15 s., a week; the weekly income of the one family may be 30 s., and that of the other only 17 s. or 18 s.

It must be admitted. however. that the workman does not retain the whole of this apparent

pecuniary advantage. The wife is taken from her household labours, and a part of increased wages is employed in purchasing, what might otherwise, be produced at home. The moral inconveniences are still greater. The infant children suffer from the want of maternal attention, and those who are older from the deficiency of religious, moral, and intellectual education, and childish relaxation and amusemcnt. The establishment of infant and Sunday schools, and laws regulating the number of hours during which children may labour, are palliatives of these evils, but they must exist. to a certain degree, whenever the labour of the wife and children is the subject of sale; and. though not, perhaps. strictly within the province of political economy. must never be omitted in any estimate of the causes affecting the welfare of the labouring classes.

The last preliminary point to which I have to call your attention is, the difference between the *rate of wages and the price of labour.*

If men were the only labourers, and if every man worked eq, lally hard, and for the same number of hours, during the year, these two expressions would be synonymous. If each man, for instance, worked three hundred days during each year, and ten hours during each day, one-three-thousandth part of each man's yearly wages would be the price of an hour's labour. But neither of these propositions is true. The yearly wages of a family often include, as we have seen, the results of the labour of the wife and children. And few things are less uniform than the number of working days during the year, or of working hours during the day, or the degree of exertion undergone during those hours.

The established annual holidays in Protestant countries; are between fifty and sixty. In many Catholic countries they exceed one hundred. Among the Hindoos, they are said to occupy nearly half the year. But these holidays are confined to a certain portion of the population; the labour of a sailor, or a soldier, or a menial servant, admits of scarcely any distinction of days.

Again, in northern and southern latitudes, the hours of out-door labour are limited by the duration of light; and in all climates by the weather. When the labouter Works under shelter, the daily hours of labour may be uniform throughout the year. And, independently of natural causes, the daily hours of labour vary in different countries, and in different employments in the same country. The daily hours of labour are, perhaps, longer in France than in England, and, certainly, are longer in England than in Hindostan. In Manchester, the manufacturer generally works twelve hours a day; in Birmingham, ten: a London shopman is seldom employed more than eight or nine.

There is still more discrepancy between the exertions made by different labours in a given period. They are often, indeed,. unsusceptible of comparison. There is no common measure of the toils undergone by a miner and a tailor, or of those of a shopman and an iron founder. And labour which is the same in kind, may vary indefinitely in intensity. Man of the witnesses examined by the Committee on Artisans and Machinery (Session of 1824) were English manufacturers, who had worked in France. They agree as to the comparative indolence of the French labourer, even during his hours of employment. One of the witnesses, Adam Young, had been two years in one of the best manufactories in Alsace. He is asked, 'Did you find the spinners there as industrious as the spinners in England?' and replies, 'No; a spinner in England will do twice as much as a Frenchman. They get up at four in the morning, and work till ten at night; but our spinners will do as much in six hours as they will in ten.'

'Had you any Frenchmen employed under you?' — 'Yes; eight, at two francs a day.'

'What had you a day?' — 'Twelve francs.'

'Supposing you had had eight English carders under you, how much more work could you have done?' — 'With one Englishman, I could have done more than I did with those eight Frenchmen. It cannot be called work they do: it is only looking at it, and wishing it done.'

'Do the French make their yarn at a greater expense?' — 'Yes; though they have their hands for much less wages than in England.' — pp. 590, 582.

Even in the same country, and in the same employments, similar inequalities are constantly observed. Every one is aware that much more exertion is undergone by the labourer by task-work than by the day-labourer; by the independent day-labourer than by the pauper; and even by the pauper than by the convict.

It is obvious that the rate of wages is less likely to be uniform than the pride of labour, as the amount of wages will be affected, in the first place, by any variations in the price, and, in the second place, by any variations in the amount, of the labour exerted.

The average annual wages of labour in England, are three times as high as in Ireland; but as the labourer in Ireland is said not to do more than one-third of what is done by the labourer in England, the price of labour may, in both countries, be about equal. In England, the labourer by task-work earns much more than the day-labourer; but as it is certainly as profitable to employ him, the price of his labour cannot be higher. It may be supposed, indeed, that the price of labour is everywhere, and at all times, the same; and, if there were no disturbing causes, — if all persons knew perfectly well their own interest, and strictly followed it, and there were no difficulties in moving capital and labour from place to place, and from employment to employment, — the price of labour, at the same time, would be everywhere the same. But these difficulties occasion the price of labour to vary materially, even at the same time and place; and variations, both in the amount of wages and in the price of labour at different times, and in different places, are occasioned, not only by these causes, but by others which will be considered in a subsequent course.

These variations affect very differently the labourer and his employer. The employer is interested in keeping down the price of labour; but while that price remains the same, while at a given expense he gets a given amount of work done, his situation remains unaltered. If a farmer can get a field trenched for £12 it is indifferent to him whether he pays the whole of that sum to three capital workmen, or to four ordinary ones. The three would receive higher wages than the four, but as they would do proportionably more work, their labour would come just as cheap. If the three could be hired at £1 10 s. a-piece, while the four required £3 a-piece, though the wages of the three would be higher, the price of the work done by them would be lower.

It is true that the causes which raise the amount of the labourer's wages often raise the rate of the capitalist's profits. It; by increased industry, one man performs the work of two, both the amount of wages and the rate of profits will generally be raised. But the rate of profit will be raised, not by the rise of wages, but in consequence of the additional supply of labour having diminished its price, or having diminished the period for which it had previously been necessary to advance that. price.

The labourer, on the other hand, is principally interested in the amount of wages. The amount of his wages being given, it is. certainly his interest that the price of his labour should be high, for on that depends the degree of exertion imposed on him. But if the amount of his wages be low, he must be comparatively poor, if that amount be high, he must be comparatively rich, whatever be his remuneration for each specific act of exertion. In the one case he will have leisure and want, — in the other, toil and abundance. I am far from thinking that the evils of severe and incessant labour, or the benefits of a certain degree of leisure, ought to be left out in any estimate of happiness. But it is not with happiness, but with wealth, that I am concerned as a political economist; and I am not only justified in omitting, but, perhaps, am bound to omit, all considerations which have no influence on wealth. In fact, however, wealth and happiness are very seldom opposed. Nature, when she imposed on man the necessity of labour, tempered his repugnance to it by making long-continued inactivity painful, and by strongly associating with exertion the idea of its reward. The poor and half-employed Irish labourer, or the still poorer and less industrious savage, is as inferior in happiness as tie is in income to the hard-worked English artisan. The Englishman's industry may sometimes be excessive, his desire to better his condition may sometimes drive him on toils productive of disease ill-recompensed by the increase of his wages, but that such is not generally the case may be proved by comparing the present duration of life in England with its former duration, or with its duration in other countries. It is generally admitted, that during the last fifty years, a marked increase has taken place in the industry of our manufacturing population, and that they are now the hardest working labourers in the world. But during the whole of that period the average duration of their lives has been constantly increasing, and appears still to increase: and notwithstanding the apparent unhealthiness of many of their occupations, notwithstanding the atmosphere of smoke and steam in which they labour for seventy-two hours a week, they enjoy longer life than the lightly-toiled inhabitants of the most favoured soils and climates. The average mortality among savage nations is the greatest that is known. In the continent of Europe it is about one in thirty-four. In England, about a century ago, when more than half of our population was agricultural, it was supposed to be one in thirty; fifty years ago it was calculated at one in forty; thirty years ago at one in forty-seven; twenty years ago at one in fifty-two. Now, when two-thirds of our labourers are manufacturers, and more than one-third dwell in cities, it is estimated at one in fifty-eight.

LECTURE II: Popular Errors on the Causes Affecting Wages

Having in the last Lecture marked the distinction which really exists between the price of labour and the amount of wages, I shall for the future consider every labouring family as consisting of the same number of persons, and exerting the same degree of industry. On that supposition, the distinction between the price of labour and the amount of wages will be at an end; or rather, the only distinction will be, that the former expression designates the remuneration for each specific exertion: the latter, the aggregate of all those separate remunerations, as summed up at the end of each year. And the question to be answered will be, what are the causes which decide what in any given country, and at any given period, shall be the quantity and quality of the commodities obtained by a labouring family during a year? The proximate cause appears to me to be clear. The quantity and quality of the commodities obtained by each labouring family during a year, must depend on the quantity and quality of the commodities directly or indirectly appropriated during the year to the use of the labouring population, compared with the number of labouring families (including under that term all those who depend on their own labour for subsistence); or, to speak more concisely, on the extent of the fund for the maintenance of labourers, compared with the number of labourers to be maintained. This proposition is so nearly self-evident, that if political economy were a new science, I should assume it without further remark. But I must warn you, that this proposition is inconsistent with opinions which are entitled to consideration, some from the number and others from the authority of those who maintain them.

First. It is inconsistent with the doctrine, that the rate of wages depends on the proportion which the number of labourers beam to the amount of *capital* in a country. The word capital has been used in so many senses, that it is difficult to state this doctrine precisely; but I know of no definition. of: that term which will not include many things that are not used by the labouring classes; and if my proposition be correct, no increase or diminution of *these* things can directly affect wages. If a foreign merchant were to come to settle in this country, and bring with him a cargo of raw and manufactured silk, lace, and diamonds, that cargo would increase the capital of the country; silks, lace, and diamonds, would become more abundant, and the enjoyments of those who use them would be increased; but the enjoyments of the labourers-would not be directly increased: indirectly, and consequentially, they might be increased. The silk might be re-exported in a manufactured state, and commodities for the use of labourers imported in return; and then, and not till then, wages would rise; but that rise would be occasioned, not by the first addition to the capital of the country, which was made in the form of silk, but by the substituted addition made in the form of commodities used by the labourer.

Secondly. It is inconsistent with the doctrine, that wages depend on the proportion borne by the number of labourers to the revenue of the society of which they are members. In the example last suggested, of the introduction of a new supply of lace or diamonds, the *revenues* of those who use lace or diamonds would be in, creased; but as wages are not spent on those articles, *they* would remain unaltered. It is possible, indeed, to state cases in which the revenue of a large portion of a community might be increased, and yet the wages of the labourers might fall without an increase of their numbers. I will suppose the principal trade of Ireland to be the raising produce for the English market; and that for every two hundred acres ten families were employed in raising, on half the land, their own subsistence, and on the remainder corn and other exportable crops requiring equal labour. Under such circumstances, if a demand should arise in the English market for cattle, butchers'-meat, and wool, instead of corn, it would be the interest of the

Irish landlords and farmers to convert their estates from arable into pasture. Instead of ten families for every two hundred acres, two might be sufficient: one to raise the subsistence of the two, and the other to tend the cattle and sheep. The revenue of the landlords and the farmers would be increased, but a large portion of the labourers would be thrown out of employment; a large portion of the land formerly employed in producing commodities for their use would be de. voted to the production of commodities for the use of England; and the fund for the maintenance of Irish labour would fall, notwithstanding the increase of the revenue of the landlords and farmers.

Thirdly. It is inconsistent with the prevalent opinion, that the non-residence of landlords, funded proprietors, mortgagees, and other unproductive consumers, can be detrimental to the labouring inhabitants of a country *that does not export raw produce.*

In a country which exports raw produce, wages may be lowered by such non-residence. If an Irish landlord resides on his estate, he requires the services of certain persons, who must also be resident there, to minister to his daily wants. He must have servants, gardeners, and perhaps gamekeepers. If he build a house, he must employ resident masons and carpenters; part of his furniture he may import, but the greater part of it must be made in his neighbourhood; a portion of his land, or, what comes to the same thing, a portion of his rent, must be employed in producing food, clothing, and shelter for all these persons, and for those who produce that food, clothing and shelter. If he were to remove to England, all these wants would be supplied by Englishmen. The land and capital which was formerly employed in providing the maintenance of Irish labourers, would be employed in producing corn and cattle to be exported to England to provide the subsistence of English labourers. The whole quantity of commodities appropriated to the use of Irish labourers would be diminished, and that appropriated to the use of English labourers increased, and wages would, consequently, rise in England, and fall in Ireland.

It is true that these effects would not be coextensive with the landlord's income. While, in Ireland, he must have consumed many foreign commodities. He must have purchased tea, wine, and sugar, and other things which the climate and the manufactures of Ireland do not afford, and he must have paid for them by sending corn and cattle to England. It is true, also, that while in Ireland he probably employed a portion of his land and of his rents for other purposes, from which the labouring population received no benefit, as a deer park, or a pleasure garden, or in the maintenance of horses or hounds. On his removal, that portion of his land which was a. park would be employed, partly in producing exportable commodities, and partly in producing subsistence for its cultivators; and that portion which fed horses for his use might be employed in feeding horses for exportation. The first of these alterations would do good; the second could do no harm. Nor must we forget that, through the cheapness of conveyance between England and Ireland, a portion, or perhaps all, of those whom he employed in Ireland might follow him to England and, in that case, wages in neither country would be affected. The fund for the maintenance of labourers in Ireland, and the number of labourers to be maintained, would both be equally diminished, and the fund for the maintenance of labourers in England, and the number of labourers to be maintained, would both be equally increased.

But after making all these deductions, and they are very great, from the supposed effect of the absenteeism of the Irish proprietors on the labouring classes in Ireland, I cannot agree with Mr. McCulloch that it is immaterial. I cannot but join in the general opinion that their return, though it would not affect the prosperity of the British empire, considered as a whole, would be immediately beneficial to Ireland, though perhaps too much importance is attached to it.

In Mr. McCulloch's celebrated examination before the committee on the state of Ireland, (4th Report, 814, Sess. 1825,)he was asked, 'Supposing the largest export of Ireland were in live cattle, and that a considerable portion of rent had been remitted in that manner, does not such a mode of producing the means of paying rent contribute less to the improvement of the poor than any extensive employment Of them in labour would produce?' — He replies, 'Unless the means of paying rent are changed when the landlord goes home, his residence can have no effect whatever.

'Would not,' he is asked, 'the population of the country be benefited by the expenditure among them of a certain portion of the rent which (if he had been absent) has (would have) been remitted (to England)?' 'No,' he replies, 'I do not see how it could be benefited in the least. If you have a certain value laid out against Irish commodities in the one case, you will have a certain value laid out against them in the other. The cattle are either exported to England, or they stay at home. If they are exported, the landlord will obtain an equivalent for them in English commodities; if they are not, he will obtain an equivalent for them in Irish commodities; so that in both cases the landlord lives on the cattle, or on the value of the cattle: and whether he lives in Ireland or in England, there is obviously just the very same amount of commodities for the people of Ireland to subsist upon.'

This reasoning assumes that the landlord, while resident in Ireland, himself personally devours all the cattle produced on his estates; for on no other supposition can there be the very same amount of commodities for the people of Ireland to subsist upon, whether their cattle are retained in Ireland or exported.

But when a country does not export raw produce, the consequences of absenteeism are very different. Those who derive their incomes from such a country cannot possibly spend them abroad until they have previously spent them at home.

When a Leicestershire landlord is resident on his estate, he employs a certain portion of his land, or, what is the same, of his rent, in maintaining the persons who provide for him those commodities and services, which must be produced on the spot where they are consumed. If he should remove to London, he would want the services of Londoners, and the produce of land and capital which previously maintained labourers resident in Leicester, would be sent away to maintain labourers resident in London. The labourers would probably follow, and wages in Leicestershire and London would then be unaltered; but until they did so, wages would rise in the one district and fall in the other. At the same time, as the rise and fall would compensate one another, as the fund for the maintenance of labour, and the number of labourers to be maintained, would each remain the same, the same amount of wages would be distributed among the same number of persons, though not precisely in the same proportion as before.

If he were now to remove to Paris, a new distribution must take place. As the price of raw produce is lower in France than in England, and the difference in habits and language between the two countries prevents the transfer of labourers from the one to the other, neither the labourers nor the produce of his estates could follow him. He must employ French labourers, and he must convert his share of the produce of his estates, or, what is the same thing, his rent into some exportable form in order to receive it abroad. It may be supposed that he would receive his rent in money. Even if he were to do so, the English labourers would not be injured, for as they do not eat or drink money, provided the same amount of commodities remained for their use, they would be unaffected by the export of money. But it is impossible that he could receive his rent in money unless tie chose to suffer a gratuitous loss. The rate of exchange between London and Paris is generally rather in favour of London, and scarcely ever so deviates from par between any two countries, as to cover the expense of transferring the precious metals from the one to the other, excepting between the countries which do, and those which do not possess mines. The remittances from England to France must be sent, therefore, in the form of manufactures, either directly to France, or to some country with which France has commercial relations. And how would these manufactures be obtained? Of course in exchange for the landlord's rent. His share of the produce of his estates would now go to Birmingham or Sheffield, or Manchester or London, to maintain the labourers employed in producing manufactures, to be sent and sold abroad for his profit. An English absentee employs his income precisely as if he were to remain at home and consume nothing but hardware and cottons. Instead of the services of gardeners and servants, upholsterers and tailors, he purchases those of spinners, and weavers, and cutlers. In either case his income is employed in maintaining labourers, though the class of labourers is different; and in either case, the whole fund for the maintenance of labourers, and the number of labourers to be maintained, remaining unaltered, the wages of labour would not be affected.

But, in fact, that fund would be rather increased in quantity and rather improved in quality. It would be increased, because land previously employed as a park, or in feeding dog's and horses, br hares and pheasants, would now be employed in producing food or clothing for men. It would be improved, because the increased production of manufactured commodities would occasion an increased division of labour, the use of more and better machinery, and the other improvements which we long ago ascertained to be its necessary accompaniments.

One disadvantage, and one only, it appears to me would be the result. The absentee in a great measure escapes domestic taxation. I say in a great measure, because he still remains liable, if a proprietor of houses or of land, to those taxes which fall upon rent: he pays, too, a part of the taxes on the materials of manufactures; and if it were our policy to tax income or exported commodities, he might be forced to pay to the public revenue even more than his former proportion. But, under our present system, which throws the bulk of taxation on commodities produced for internal consumption, he receives the greater part of his revenue without deduction, and. instead of contributing to the support of the British Government, contributes to support that. of France or Italy. This inconvenience, perhaps, about balances the advantages which I have just mentioned, and leaves a community which exports only manufactures, neither impoverished nor enriched by the residence abroad of its unproductive members.

I ought, perhaps, on this occasion again to remind you, that it is to wealth and poverty that my attention is confined. The *moral* effects of absenteeism must never be neglected by a writer who inquires into the causes which promote the *happiness* of nations, but are without the province of a political economist. Nor do I regret that, they are so, for they form a subject on which it is far more difficult to obtain satisfactory results. In one respect, indeed, the moral question is the more simple, as it is not complicated by the consideration whether raw produce or manufactures are exported, or whether the non-resident landlord is abroad, or in some town within his own country. If his presence is to be morally beneficial it must be his presence on his own estate. To the inhabitants of that estate, the place to which he absents himself is indifferent. Adam Smith believed his residence to be morally injurious. The residence of a court, he observes (book ii. chap. 3), 'in general makes the inferior sort of people dissolute and poor. The inhabitants of a large village, after having made considerable progress in manufactures, have become idle in consequence of a great lord having taken up his residence in their neighbourhood.' And Mr. M'Culloch, whose fidelity and intelligence as an observer may be relied on, states, as the result of his own experience, that in Scotland the estates of absentees are almost always the best managed. Much, of coarse, depends on individual character; but I am inclined to believe that in general the presence of men of large fortune is morally detrimental, and that of men of moderate fortune morally beneficial, to their immediate neighbourhood. The habits of expense and indulgence which, in different gradations, prevail among all the. members of a great establishment, are mischievous as. examples, and perhaps still more so as sources of repining and discontent.. The drawing room and stable do harm to the neighbouring gentry, and the housekeeper's room and servants' hall to their. inferiors. But families of moderate income, including under that term incomes between 500 l, and 2000 l, a year, appear to be placed in the station most favourable to the acquisition of moral anal intellectual excellence, and to its diffusion among their associates and dependents. I have no doubt that a well-regulated gentleman's family, removing. the prejudices, soothing the quarrels, directing and stimulating the exertions, and awarding praise or blame to the conduct of the villagers round them, is among the most efficient means by which the character of a neighbourhood can be improved.. It is the happiness of this country, that. almost every parish has a resident fitted by fortune and, education for these services; and bound, not merely by feelings of propriety, but as a matter of express and professional duty, to their performance. The dispersion throughout the country of so many thousand clerical families, each acting in its own district as a small centre of civilization, is an advantage to which, perhaps, we have been too long accustomed to be able to appreciate its extent.

Still, however, I think that even the moral effects of absenteeism have been exaggerated. Those who declaim against the 12,000 English families supposed to be resident abroad, seem to forget that not one-half, probably not onequarter, of them, if they were to return, would dwell anywhere but in towns, where their influence would be wasted, or probably not even exerted. What does it signify to the Connaught, or Northumbrian, or Devonshire peasant, whether his landlord lives in Dublin, or London, or Cheltenham, or Rome? And even of those who would reside in the country, how many would exercise that influence beneficially? How many would be fox-hunters or game-preservers, or surround themselves with dependents whose example would more than compensate for the virtues of their masters? Nothing can be more rash than to predict that good would be the result of causes which are quite as capable of producing evil.

The economical effects have been still more generally misunderstood; and I have often been tempted to wonder that doctrines so clear as those which I have been submitting to you, should be admitted with reluctance even by those who feel the proofs to be unanswerable, and should be rejected at once by others, as involving a paradox too monstrous to be worth examination.

Much of this, probably, arises from a confusion of the economical with the moral part of the question. Many writers and readers of political economy forget that wealth only is within the province of that science; and that the clearest proof that absenteeism diminishes the virtue or the happiness of the remaining members of a community is no answer to arguments which aim only at proving that it does not diminish their wealth.

Another source of error arises from the circumstance, that when the landlord is present, the gain is concentrated, and the loss diffused; when he is absent, the gain is diffused, and the loss concentrated. When he quits his estate, we can put our finger on the village tradesman and labourer who lose his custom and employment. We cannot trace the increase of custom and employment that is consequently scattered among millions of manufacturers. When he returns, we see that the expenditure of £2000 or £3000 a year in a small circle gives wealth and spirit to its inhabitants. We do not see, however clearly we may infer it, that so much the less is expended in Manchester, Birmingham, or Leeds. The inhabitants of his village attribute their gain and their loss to its causes; and their complaints and acknowledgments are loud in proportion to the degree in which they feel their interests to be affected. No single manufacturer is conscious that the average annual export of more than forty millions sterling has been increased or diminished to the amount of two or three thousand pounds. And even if aware of that increase or diminution, he would not attribute it to the residence in Yorkshire or Paris of a given individual, of whose existence he probably is not aware. When to obvious and palpable effects nothing is to be opposed but inferences deduced by a long, though perfectly demonstrative reasoning process, no one can doubt which will prevail, both with the uneducated and the educated vulgar.

Many persons, also, are perplexed by the consideration, that all the commodities which are exported as remittances of the absentee's income are exports for which no return is obtained; that they are as much lost to this country as if they were a tribute paid to a: foreign state, or even as if they were thrown periodically into the sea. This is unquestionably true; but it must be recollected, that whatever is unproductively consumed, is, by the very terms of the proposition, destroyed, without producing any return. The only difference between the two cases is, that the resident landlord performs that destruction here; the absentee performs it abroad. In either case, he first purchases the services of those Who produce the things which he for his benefit, not for theirs, is to consume. If he stays here, lie pays a man to brush a coat, or clean a pair of boots, or arrange a table — all which in an hour after are in their former condition. When abroad, he pays an equal sum for the production of needles, or calicoes, which are sent abroad, and equally consumed without further benefit to those who produced them. The income of unproductive consumers, however paid. is a tribute; and whether they enjoy it here or elsewhere, is their own concern. We know that a man cannot eat his cake and have it; and itis equally true that he cannot sell a- cake to another and keep it for himself.

The last cause to which I attribute the slow progress of correct opinions on this subject, is their distastefulness to the most influential members of the community. Nothing can be more flattering to landlords, annuitants, mortgagees, and fundholders, than to be told that their residence is of vital importance to the country. Nothing can be more humiliating than to be assured that it is utterly immaterial to the rest of the community whether they live in Brighton, or London, or Paris. Those who are aware how much our judgment, even in matters of science, is influenced by our wishes, will not be surprised at the prejudices against a doctrine which forbids the bulk of the educated class to believe that they are benefactors to their country. by the mere act of residing within its shores.

I may appear, perhaps, to have dwelt too much on a single subject; but no prevalent error can be effectually exposed until its prevalence has been accounted for. And these arc errors which are to be heard in every society, and often from those whose general views in political economy are correct. They may be called harmless errors, but no error is, in fact, harmless; and when there is so much in our habits that really requires alteration, we may lose sight of the real and the remediable causes of evil, while our attention is misdirected to absenteeism.

LECTURE III: Popular Errors On the Causes Affecting Wages, (concluded.)

I stated in the last Lecture, that the quantity and quality of the commodities obtained by each labouring family during the year, must depend on the quantity and quality of the commodities directly or indirectly appropriated during the year to the use of the labouring population, compared with the number of labouring families; or, to speak more concisely, on the extent of the fund for the maintenance of labourers, compared with the number of labourers to be maintained; and I observed, that this proposition is inconsistent with many opinions entitled to consideration. Three of those opinions I then examined; in the present Lecture I shall consider the remainder.

Fourthly. It is inconsistent with the doctrine that the general rate of wages can, except in two cases, be diminished by the introduction of machinery.

The two cases in which the introduction of machinery can produce such an effect, are first, when labour is employed in the construction of machinery, which labour would otherwise have been employed in the production of commodities for the use of labourers; and, secondly, when the machine itself consumes commodities which would otherwise have been consumed by labourers, and that to a greater extent than it produces them.

The first case is put by Mr. Ricardo, in his chapter on Machinery; but in so detailed a form, that, instead of reading it, I will extract its substance, with a slight variation of the terms. He supposes a capitalist to carry on the business of a manufacturer of commodities for the use of labourers; or, to use a more concise expression, the business of a manufacturer of wages. He supposes him to have been in the habit of commencing every year with a capital consisting of wages for a certain number of labourers, which we call twenty-six, and of employing that capital in hiring twenty men, to reproduce, during the year, wages for the whole twenty-six, and six to produce commodities for himself. He now supposes him to employ ten of his men during a year in producing, not wages, but a machine, which, with the aid of seven men to keep it in repair and work it, will produce every year wages for thirteen men. At the end of the year the capitalist's situation would be unaltered: he would have wages for thirteen men, the produce of the labour of his other ten men during the year — and his machine, also the produce of the labour of ten men during the year, and therefore of equal value. And his situation would *continue* unaltered. Every year his machine would produce wages for thirteen men, of whom seven must be employed in repairing and working it, and six might, as before, be employed for the benefit of the capitalist. But we have seen that, during the year in which the machine was constructed, only ten men were employed in producing wages instead of twenty, and, consequently, that wages were produced for only thirteen men instead of for twenty-six. At the end of that year, therefore, the fund for the maintenance of labour was diminished, and wages must consequently, have fallen. It is of great importance to recollect, that the only reason for this fall was the diminution of the annual production. The twenty men produced wages for twenty-six men: the machine produces wages for only thirteen. The vulgar error on this subject supposes the evil to arise, not from. its true-cause, the expense of constructing the machine, but from the productive powers of that machine. So far is this from being true, that those productive powers are the specific benefit which is to be set against the evil of its expensiveness. If, instead of wages for thirteen men, the machine could produce wages for thirty, its use, as soon as it came into operation, would have increased instead of diminishing the fund for the maintenance of labour. The same effect would have been produced, if the machine could have been obtained without expense; or, if the capitalist, instead of building it out of his capital, had built it out of his profits — if, instead of withdrawing ten men for a year from the production of wages, he had employed in its construction, during two years, five of the men whom he is supposed to have employed in producing commodities for his own use. In either case, the additional produce obtained from the machine would have been an additional fund for the maintenance of labour; and wages must, according to my elementary proposition, have risen.[3]

I have thought it necessary to state this possible evil as a part of the theory of machinery, but I am far from attaching any practical importance to it. I do not believe that there exists upon record a single instance in which the whole annual produce has been diminished by the use of *inanimate* machinery. Partly in consequence of the expense of constructing the greater part of machinery being defrayed out of profits or rent, and partly in consequence of the great proportion which the productive powers of machinery bear to the expense of its construction, its use is uniformly accompanied by an enormous increase of production. The annual consumption of cotton wool in this country, before the introduction of the spinning jenny, did not amount to 100,000 lbs.; it now amounts to 190,000,000. Since the power-loom came into use, the quantity of cotton cloth manufactured for home consumption has increased from 227,000,000 of yards (the average annual amount between the years 1816 and 1820), to 400,000,000 of yards (the annual average from 1824 to 1828 (Huskisson's Speech, 1830). The number of copies of books extant at any one period before the invention of the printing-press, was probably smaller than that which is now produced in a single day. Mr. Ricardo's proposition, therefore (Princ. 474), that the use of machinery frequently diminishes the quantity of the gross produce of a country, is. erroneous, so far as it depends on the case which he has supposed, and of which I have stated the substance.

The other exception, that where the machine itself consumes commodities which would otherwise have been consumed by labourers, and that to a greater extent than it produces them, applies only to the case of horses and working cattle, which may be termed animated machines. We will suppose a farmer to employ on his farm twenty men, who produce annually their own subsistence, and that of six other men producing commodities for the use of their master. if five horses, consuming, we will say, as much as eight men, could do the work of ten, it would be worth the farmer's while to substitute them for eight of his men, as he would be able to increase the number of persons who work for his own benefit from six to eight. But after deducting the subsistence of the horses, the fund for the maintenance of labourers would be reduced from wages for twenty-six men to wages for eighteen. I cannot refuse to admit that such cases may exist, or to deplore the misery that must accompany them. They are, in fact, now occurring in Ireland, and are occasioning much of the distress of that country. They seem, indeed, to be the natural accompaniments of a certain period in the progress of national improvement. In the early stages of society, the rank and even the safety of the landed proprietor is principally determined by the number of his dependents. The best mode of increasing that number is to allow the land, which he does not occupy as his own demesne, to be subdivided into small tenements, each cultivated by one family, and just sufficient for their support. Such tenants can of course pay little rent, but they arc enabled by their abundant leisure, and forced by their absolute dependence, to swell the retinue, and aid the political influence, of their landlord in peace, and to follow his banner in public and private war. Cameron of Lochiel, whose rental did not exceed £500 a year, carried with him into the rebellion of 1745, eight hundred men raised from his own tenantry. But in the progress of civilization, as wealth becomes the principal means of distinction and influence, landowners prefer rent to dependents. To obtain rent, that. process of cultivation must be employed which will give, not absolutely the greatest amount of produce, but the greatest after deducting the expenses. For this purpose a tract of five hundred acres, from which fifty families produced their own subsistence, and produced scarcely anything more, may be converted into one farm, and with the labour of ten families, and as many horses, may produce the subsistence of only thirty families. Fortunately, however, the period at which these alterations take place is generally one of great social improvement; so that, after a short interval, the increased diligence and skill with which labour is applied, occasion an increase of even the gross produce. The fund for the maintenance of labourers now becomes increased from two different sources — partly from the increased efficiency of human labour. when aided by that of horses and cattle, and partly from the results of a part of the human labour set free by the substitution of brutes. The ultimate consequences of such a change are always beneficial; the change. itself must, in general, be accompanied by distress.

But with the exception of these two cases, one of which produces only temporary effects, and the other, though :apparently possible, seem never actually to occur, it. appears to me dear that the use. of machinery must either rase the general rate of wages, or leave it unaltered.

When machinery is applied to the production of commodities which are not intended, directly or indirectly, for the use of labourers, it occasions no alteration in the general rate of wages; — I say the general rate of wages; because it may diminish the rate of wages in some employments, — a diminution. always compensated by a corresponding increase in some others. I was shown at Birmingham a small screw, which, in the manufacture of corkscrews, performed the work of fifty-nine men; with its assistance one man could cut a spiral groove in as many corkscrew shanks as sixty men could have cut in the same time with the tools previously in use. As the use of corkscrews is limited, it is not probable that the demand for them has sufficiently increased to enable the whole number of labourers previously employed in their manufacture, to remain so employed after such an increase in their productive power. Some of the corkscrew-makers, therefore, must have been thrown out of work, and the rate of wages in that trade probably fell. But as the whole fund for the maintenance of labourers, and the whole number of labourers to be maintained, remained unaltered, that fall must have been balanced by a rise somewhere else — a rise which we may trace to its proximate cause, by recollecting that the fall in the price of corkscrews must have left every purchaser of a corkscrew a fund for the purchase of labour, rather larger than he would have possessed if he had paid the former price.

If, however, machinery be applied to the production of any commodity used by the labouring population, the general rate of wages will rise. That it cannot fall is clear, on the grounds which I have just stated. If the improvement be great, and the commodity not subject to a corresponding increase of demand, some of the labourers formerly employed in its production will be thrown out of employment, and wages, in that trade, will fall — a fall which, as the whole fund for the maintenance of labour is not diminished, must be met by a corresponding rise in some other trade. But the fund *will be increased* by the additional quantity produced of the commodity to which the improvement has been applied: estimated in that commodity, therefore, the general rate of wages, or, in other words, the quantity of commodities obtained by the labouring population, will be increased by the introduction of machinery; estimated in all others, it will be stationary.

The example taken from the manufacture of corkscrews is as unfavourable to the effects of machinery as can be proposed; for the use of the commodity is supposed to be unable to keep up with the increased production, and the whole number of labourers employed on it is, consequently, diminished. This, however, is a very rare occurrence. The usual effect of an increase in the facility of producing a commodity is so to increase its consumption as to occasion the employment of more, not less, labour than before.

I have already called your attention to the effects of machinery in the manufacture of cotton and in printing. Each of these trades probably employs ten times as many labourers as it would have employed if spinning-jennies and types had not been invented. Under such circumstances (and they are the usual ones), the benefits of machinery are not alloyed by even partial inconvenience.

Fifthly. Closely connected with this mistake, and occasioned by the same habit of attending only to what is temporary and partial, and neglecting what is permanent and general; of dwelling on the evil that is concentrated, and being insensible of the benefit that is diffused, is the common error of supposing that the general rate of wages can be reduced by the importation of foreign commodities. In fact the opening of a new market is precisely analogous to the introduction of a new machine, except that it is a machine which it costs nothing to construct or to keep up. If the foreign commodity be not consumed by the labouring population, its introduction leaves the general rate of wages unaffected; if it be used by them, their wages are raised as estimated in that commodity. If the absurd laws which favour the wines of Portugal to the exclusion of those of France were repealed, more labourers would be employed in producing commodities for the French market, and fewer for the Portuguese. Wages would temporarily fall in the one trade, and rise in the other. The clear benefit would be derived by the drinkers of wine, who, at the same expense, would obtain more and better wine. So if what arc called the protecting duties on French silks were removed, fewer labourers would be employed in the direct production of silk, and more in its indirect production, by the production of the cottons, or hardware, with which it would be purchased. The wearers of silk would be the only class ultimately benefited; and as the labouring population neither wear silk nor drink wine, the general rate of wages would, in both cases, remain unaltered. But if the laws which prohibit our obtaining on the most advantageous terms tea, and sugar, and corn, were altered, that portion of the. fund for the maintenance of labour, which consists of corn, sugar, and tea, would be increased. And the general rate of wages, as estimated in the three most important articles of food, would be raised.

Sixthly. The views which I have been endeavouring to explain, are inconsistent with the common opinion, that the unproductive consumption of landlords and capitalists is beneficial to the labouring classes, because it furnishes them with *employment*. The maintainers of this theory must forget that it is not employment, but food, clothing, shelter, and fuel — in short, the materials of subsistence and comfort, that the labouring classes require. The word employment is merely a concise form of designating toil, trouble, exposure, and fatigue. All these, per se, are evils, and the less of them that is required for obtaining a given amount of subsistence and comfort, — or, in other words, the greater the facility of obtaining that given amount, — the better, *caeteris paribus*, will be the condition of the labouring classes; indeed, of all classes in the community. What occasions the prosperity of a colony? Not the dearness of subsistence, but its cheapness; not the difficulty of obtaining food, clothing; shelter, and fuel, but the facility. Now how can unproductive consumption increase this facility? How can the fund from which all are to be maintained be augmented by the destruction of a portion of it? If the higher orders were to return to the customs of a century ago, and cover their coats with gold lace, they might enjoy their own finery; but how would that benefit their inferiors? The theory which I am considering, replies that they would be benefited by being *employed* in making the lace. It is true that a coat, instead of costing £5, would cost £55 But what becomes *now* of the extra £50? for it cannot be said that because it is not spent on a laced coat, it does not exist. If a landlord with £10,000 a year spends it unproductively, he pays it away to those who furnish the embellishments of his house and grounds, and supply his stable, his equipage, and his clothes. Suppose him now to abandon all unproductive expenditure, to confine himself to bare necessaries, and to earn them by his own labour, the first consequence would be, that those among whom he previously spent his £10,000 a year would lose him as an employer; and beyond this the theory in question sees nothing. But what would he do with the £10,000 which he would still annually receive? No one supposes that he would lock it up in a box, or bury it in his garden. Whether productively or unproductively, it still must be spent. If spent by himself, as by the supposition it would be spent productively, it must increase, and every year still further increase the whole fund applicable to the use of the rest of the community. If not spent by himself, it must be lent to some other person, and by that person it must be spent productively or unproductively. He might, perhaps, buy with it property in the English funds; but what becomes of it in the hands of the person who sells to him that funded property? He might buy with it French rentes; but in what form would the price of those rentes go to Paris? — In the form, as we have seen, of manufactured commodities. *Quacunque via data*, every man must spend his income; and the less he spends on himself, the more remains for the rest of the world.

The last theory, inconsistent with my own views, to which I shall call your attention, is that proposed by Mr. Ricardo in the following passage: —

'The labouring class have no small interest in the manner in which the net income of the country is expended, although it should, in all cases, be expended for the gratification and enjoyment of those who are fairly entitled to it.

'If a landlord, or a capitalist, expends his revenue in the manner of an ancient baron, in the support of a great number of retainers or menial servants, he will give employment to much more labour than if he expended it on fine clothes or costly furniture.

'In both cases the net revenue would be the same, and so would be the gross revenue, but the former would be realized in different commodities. If my revenue were £10,000, the same quantity nearly of productive labour would be employed, whether I realized it in fine clothes and costly furniture, etc.

etc., or in a quantity of food and clothing of the same value. If, however, I realized my revenue in the first set of commodities, no more labour would be consequently employed: I should enjoy my furniture and my clothes, and there would be an end of them; but if I realized my revenue in food and clothing, and my desire was to employ menial servants, all those whom I could so employ with my revenue of £10,000, or with the food and clothing which it would purchase, would be to be added to the former demand for labourers, and this addition would take place only because I chose this mode of expending my revenue. As the labourers, then, are interested in the demand for labour, they must naturally desire that as much as possible should be diverted from expenditure on luxuries, to be expended in the support of menial servants.

In the same manner a country engaged in war, and which is under the necessity of main mining large fleets and armies, employs a great many more men than will be employed when the war terminates, and the annual expenses which it brings with it cease.

If I were not called upon for a tax of £500 during the war, which is expended on men in the situations of soldiers and sailors, I might probably spend that portion of my income on furniture, clothes, books, etc. etc., and whether it was expended in the one way or the other, there would be the same quantity of labour employed in production; for the food and clothing of the soldier and sailor would require the same amount of industry to produce them as the more luxurious commodities: but, in the case of war, there would be the additional demand for men as soldiers and sailors; and, consequently, a war which is supported out of the revenue, and not from the capital of a country, is favourable to an increase of population.

At the termination of the war, when part of my revenue reverts to me, and is employed as before in the purchase of wine, furniture, or other luxuries, the population which it before supported, and which the war called into existence, will become redundant, and by its effect on the rest of the population, and its competition with it for employment, will sink the value of wages, and very materially deteriorate the condition of the labouring classes.'[4]

Mr. Ricardo's theory is, that it is more beneficial to the labouring classes to be employed in the production of services than in the production of commodities; that it is better for them to be employed in standing behind chairs than in making chairs; as soldiers or sailors than as manufacturers. Now as it is clear that the whole quantity of commodities provided for the use of labourers is not increased by the conversion of an artisan into a footman or a soldier, either Mr. Ricardo must be wrong, or my elementary proposition is false.

Mr. Ricardo seems to have been led to his conclusions by observing that the wages of servants, sailors, and soldiers are principally paid in kind — those of artisans in money. He correctly states, that if a man with £10,000-a-year spends his income in the purchase of commodities for his own use, he retains, after having made those purchases, no further fund for the maintenance of labour; but that if he spends it in the purchase of commodities to be employed in maintaining menial servants, he has, in those purchased commodities, a new fund with which he can maintain a certain number of menial servants. It appeared to him, therefore, that the landlord would, in the latter case, be able to spend his income twice over; to subsist twice as many persons as before. It did not occur to him that the landlord, by purchasing himself the subsistence of his servants, merely does for them what they would be able to do better for themselves; that, instead of spending his own income twice over, he merely takes on himself the business of spending theirs for them;[5] and that if he were to give to his servants the value of their whole subsistence in money, the whole body of labourers would be just as well maintained as in the supposed case of his purchasing their subsistence, and then giving it to them in exchange for their services. No one would maintain that if it were the practice, in this country, as it is in India, to give to servants board wages, the demand for labour would be lessened; or that if it were the practice, as it is in semi-barbarous countries, to maintain servants to produce within their masters walls the commodities which we are accustomed to purchase from shops, the demand for labour would be increased. Still less could it be. maintained, that if those servants, instead of producing commodities, were employed in following their master's person, or mounting guard before his door, such a change would create an additional demand for men, and be favourable to an increase of population.

So far am I from concurring in Mr. Ricardo's opinion, that it is the interest of the labourers that revenue should be spent rather on service s than on commodities, that I believe their interest to be precisely opposite. In the first place, the labourer can generally manage better his own income than it can be managed for him by his master. If a domestic servant could earn as wages the whole sum which he costs his master, even if he were to spend it as he received it, he would probably spend it with more enjoyment. Secondly, the income spent on services is spent in the purchase of what perishes at the instant of its creation; that spent on commodities often leaves results which, when their first purchaser has done with them, are serviceable to others. In this country the poor are, to a great extent, clothed with garments originally provided for their superiors. In all the better class of cottages may be found articles of furniture which never could have been made for their present possessors. A large portion of the commodities which now contribute to the comfort of the labouring classes would never have existed, if it had been the fashion in this country, during the last fifty years, to prefer retinue and attendance to durable commodities. And, thirdly, the income employed on commodities is favourable to the creation of both material and immaterial capital; that employed on services is not. The duties of a servant are so easily learned, that he can scarcely be termed a skilled labourer: his accumulations are small in amount, and seldom turned to much advantage. The artisan learns a trade, in which every year adds to his skill, and is taught mechanical and chemical processes, often susceptible of indefinite improvement, and in which a single invention may raise the author to wealth, and diffuse prosperity over a whole district, or even a whole nation. An industrious artisan can often save a large portion of his income, and invest it with great and immediate profit. He purchases with his savings a small stock of tools and materials, and by the vigilance and activity which can be applied only to a small capital, renders every portion of it efficient. The ancestors, and not the remote ancestors, of some of our richest and our proudest families, the authors of some of our most valuable discoveries, were common mechanics. What menial servant has in this country, and in modern times, been a public benefactor, or even raised himself to affluence? Both history and observation show that those countries in which expenditure is chiefly employed in the purchase of services are poor, and those in which it is employed on commodities are rich.

Mr. Ricardo's theory as to the effects of war is still more strikingly erroneous. It is, in the first place, open to all the objections which I have already opposed to his views respecting menial servants. The revenue which is employed in maintaining soldiers and sailors would, even if unproductively consumed, maintain at least an equal number of servants and artisans; and that portion of it which would have been employed in the maintenance of artisans would (as we have seen) have been far more beneficially employed. The demand for soldiers and sailors is not, as he terms it, an additional, it is merely a substituted demand. But a great part of that revenue would have been productively consumed. Instead of employing some labourers in converting suburbs into fortifications, and forests into navies, to perish by dry rot in harbour, or by exposure, at sea, and others in walking the deck and parading on the rampart, it would have employed them in adding more and more every year to the fund from which their subsistence is derived. War is mischievous to every class in the community; but to none is it such. a curse as to the labourers.

THE END.

Notes

3. And yet it appears now to be thought, that wages may be raised by the destruction or (what is the same in immediate effect) the disuse of machines already constructed.
4. Principles, etc., p. 475.
5. He did not perceive that all that the landlord spends in purchasing the subsistence and clothing of his servants is so much deducted from what he would otherwise have to pay them in money.

Also available from the publisher:

Selected Works of Salvador Allende

Ethics of Socialism – Ernest Belfort Bax

Twenty Years in Underground Russia – Cecilia Bobrovskaya

The Decline of American Capitalism – Lewis Corey

Imperialism and the Revolution – Enver Hoxha

The Selected Works of Kim Il Sung

The Stalin Era – Anna Louise Strong

Selected Works: Volume 1 – Joseph Stalin

Selected Works: Volume 2 – Joseph Stalin

www.PrismKeyPress.com

www.ingramcontent.com/pod-product-compliance
Lightning Source LLC
Chambersburg PA
CBHW071640170526
45166CB00003B/1370